Eridu: The History and Legacy of the Oldest City in Ancient Mesopotamia

By Charles River Editors

An imagined depiction of the port at Eridu

About Charles River Editors

Charles River Editors is a boutique digital publishing company, specializing in bringing history back to life with educational and engaging books on a wide range of topics. Keep up to date with our new and free offerings with this 5 second sign up on our weekly mailing list, and visit Our Kindle Author Page to see other recently published Kindle titles.

We make these books for you and always want to know our readers' opinions, so we encourage you to leave reviews and look forward to publishing new and exciting titles each week.

Introduction

A picture of the ruins of Eridu

Eridu

"After the kingship descended from heaven, the kingship was in Eridu." – Excerpt from the opening paragraph of the Sumerian King List

Emerging from the desert flats of southern Iraq can be seen the remains of a large mound, approximately 1750 feet x 1750 feet in size, surrounded by several smaller mounds. Known today as Tell Abu Shahrain or in the ancient world as Eridu, this site contains some of best examples of the Ubaid culture, and it was one of the first urban centers of civilization in southern Mesopotamia, if not the first itself.

Many famous stories came from the mythical landscapes of Iraq's deep south. In the literature of ancient Sumer, Eridu was regarded as the primordial city, the first urban center, believed to have existed long before the great mythical Flood that wiped out human culture in the Book of Genesis and other earlier traditions. It was to places like this that Western explorers first came in the 19th century, searching for the origins of the lands which the Bible described as the cradle of the human race. In doing so, they discovered that Eridu was also a real place.

The astonishing site is located about 8 miles southwest of the Sumerian city of Ur, and when it was first excavated in the mid-19th century, Western archaeologists were confused as to how a city as large as this could have existed in such a vast and waterless desert. But Eridu is positioned on the edge of the great alluvial plain of Sumer, a wild and beautiful marshland where the Tigris and the Euphrates meet. This was the Biblical "Garden of Eden", an ancient landscape that was renowned for its fertility in the past.

To many Westerners, Iraq's history and culture were a blank before 1991, but ironically, as war engulfed the region, it helped underscore the importance and influence of the area on Western civilization. It was here, in the ferocious landscape of south Iraq, old Sumer, that the first laws, science, and cities came into being. Eridu is a place of extraordinary significance for the study of the earliest stages of civilization in history, and it is one of the best examples of cultural continuity in Mesopotamia, from the earliest prehistoric stages in which settlements emerged to the later historic periods. Eridu had a special status, not as the residence of a ruling dynasty of kings but for its religious significance; a series of temples were built there, devoted to the patron god of the city, Enki. Each one was built upon the ruins of its predecessor, and each one represents the architectural, religious, and social changes that occurred at the site throughout its history.

Eridu: The History and Legacy of the Oldest City in Ancient Mesopotamia examines the tumultuous history of one of the most important cities of antiquity. Along with pictures depicting important people, places, and events, you will learn about Eridu like never before.

Eridu: The History and Legacy of the Oldest City in Ancient Mesopotamia
About Charles River Editors
Introduction
   Prehistoric Mesopotamia
   The Location and Landscape of Eridu
   The Mythological City of Eridu
   The Great Flood
   Linking Myth to History
   Ceramic Production
   Religion
   The Decline of Eridu
   Eridu in the Modern Age
   Online Resources
   Bibliography
Free Books by Charles River Editors
Discounted Books by Charles River Editors

Prehistoric Mesopotamia

The word Mesopotamia highlights the central theme of life in the Fertile Crescent, coming from the ancient Greek for "land between two rivers".[1] These rivers were the Tigris and the Euphrates, which both rise in the Taurus Mountains of Anatolia and flow through present-day Syria and Iraq and into the Persian Gulf. Civilization was born on the banks of these two rivers, and the sediment that was carried by the fast-flowing waters of the Anatolian highlands gradually settled as it reached Iraq as it became calmer. Seasonal floods distributed the nutrient-rich sediment along the river banks all the way to the Persian Gulf, creating an alluvial plain where irrigation could flourish.[2]

The people who settled in Mesopotamia were inextricably connected to their environmental context. In central and southern Mesopotamia the low hills and fertile plains were juxtaposed with swamps, jungles, and countless streams where the Tigris and Euphrates drained into the Persian Gulf – most of which have disappeared over the course of time.[3] Water was vital for farming, drinking, and transport across the region. It facilitated trade and communication between complementary economic spheres.[4] Mesopotamia had few natural resources; no stone, wood, or precious metals could be found in southern Iraq. There was only water, and a rich alluvial soil with which a hardworking people could transform a land of scarcity into a land of plenty.

The Mesopotamian civilizations are amongst the world's oldest, with archaeological evidence stretching back beyond 6000 BCE into the Neolithic. As hunter-gatherers discovered ways to farm and store their food for weeks and months at a time, instead of being itinerant they decided to colonize lands along the fertile banks of the Tigris and Euphrates. During the Ubaid Period (ca. 6500 – 3800 BCE), the earliest settlements were established in southern Mesopotamia.[5] Thanks to a number of technological breakthroughs, including the adoption of the wheel, the mass-production of mud bricks, and irrigation, the people of Mesopotamia managed to successfully reside at single locations for generations, and over time, their settlements grew in size and formed so-called "tell" sites.[6] Many of the smaller villages were clustered in relatively close proximity to one another due to the nature of irrigation on the alluvial plain. The large

---

[1] Polybius (2012) *Polybius: The Histories.* Chicago: University of Chicago
[2] Wilkinson, T. J. (2000) "Regional approaches to Mesopotamian archaeology: the contribution of archaeological surveys." *Journal of Archaeological Research*, 8:3. 219–267.
[3] Bahrani, Z. (1998) "Conjuring Mesopotamia: Imaginative Geography a World Past." in Meskell, L. *Archaeology under Fire: Nationalism, Politics and Heritage in the Eastern Mediterranean and Middle East.* London: Routledge. 159–174
[4] Bahrani, 1998
[5] Bogucki, P. (1990) *The Origins of Human Society.* Malden: Blackwell
[6] A "tell" is the name given to an ancient city that resembles a mound, due to the stacked layers of ruined mud-brick architecture formed by generations of inhabitation.

cities would have had a number of smaller satellite towns in their hinterland. The archaeological remains of the latter have largely disappeared over time, so it is large sites like Eridu that archaeologists must look at to build a picture of life in ancient Mesopotamia.

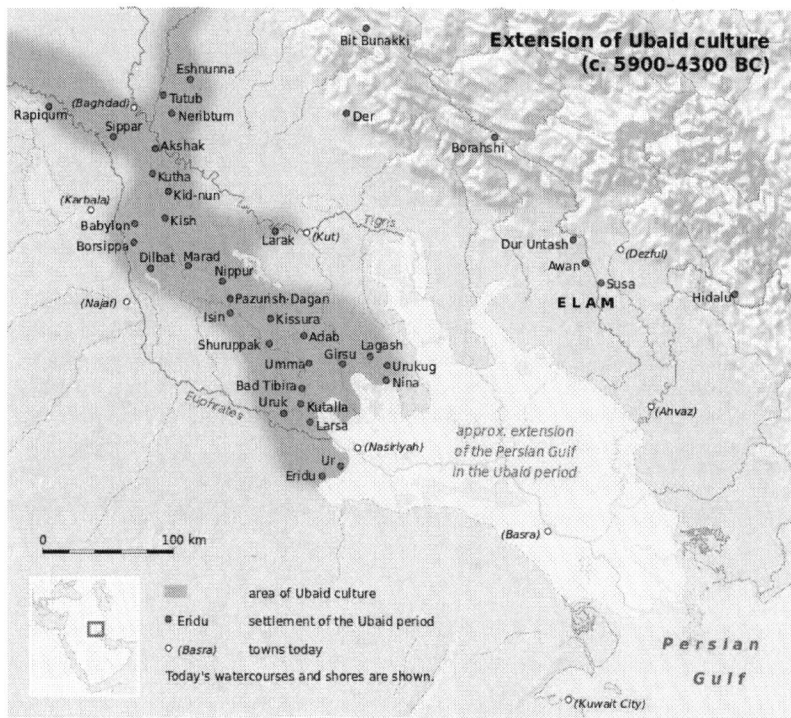

John D. Croft's map of the region, with Eridu at bottom

The bulk of Mesopotamia is in what is now Iraq, but in ancient times this land was divided between two broad groups, the Sumerians and the Akkadians. The Sumerians lived in the south and spoke their own unique language. The Akkadians to the north, by contrast, were Semites who spoke a language whose modern relatives include Hebrew and Arabic. The Sumerians were able farmers who dug ditches to divert the life-giving waters of the Tigris and Euphrates to their fields, and thanks to the abundant food supply brought by their ingenuity, they flourished. Sumerian city-states grew to a size of many hundreds of thousands of people, each being organized around the worship of an individual deity associated with the temple of the main city.[7]

The semi-nomadic Sumerian culture arrived in Mesopotamia in the middle of the 4th millennium BCE, and they eventually came to dominate the southern part of the region, though their origins before they moved into Mesopotamia remain shrouded in mystery. Their culture became concentrated in the major urban centers of the region, namely Eridu, Ur, Uruk, Larsa, and Nippur, but they were not the only residents of southern Mesopotamia. Early villages were composed of settlers from many different regions, many with their own distinctive characteristics that differed from those of the Sumerians. Some have argued that it was these cultural differences that contributed to the many technological inventions and innovations that occurred in Mesopotamia in the formative stages of urbanization.[8] It also partly explains the complexity of the region's religious systems.

The Sumerians were great inventors, and none of their inventions was more important than writing. Writing systems emerged at an early stage in the mid-4th millennium BCE, first through pictographs and later by the cuneiform script. Cuneiform became the most dominant form of writing across the region, the letters of which were pressed into clay tablets with a triangular stylus, and it is thanks to this writing system that scholars have been able to reconstruct life in ancient Mesopotamia in such vivid detail.

---

[7] Lloyd, S. (1978) *The Archaeology of Mesopotamia: From the Old Stone Age to the Persian Conquest*. London: Thames and Hudson. .
[8] Simons, G. (2016) *Iraq: From Sumer to Saddam*. Springer.

A pottery jar from the Ubaid Period

In this world of almost unlimited potential, the Book of Genesis said that the first cities arose in the beginning, when God let dry land rise from the water, but the Bible was not the earliest of such narratives. According to the Sumerians' own myths, in the beginning, there was the city of Eridu.

The Location and Landscape of Eridu

Eridu is one of the southernmost cities of Mesopotamia, located approximately 8 miles southwest of Ur. Four miles to the west is the small site of Tell el-'Obeid, where a great number of Sumerian finds have also been discovered. Within and around the L-shaped structure upon the mound, four life-size copper lion heads have been discovered, as well as several others of different sizes resembling panthers and other felines.[9] The other largest cities in the region were Ur and Uruk, but they would only overtake Eridu in size and importance after Eridu began to decline towards the end of the 3rd millennium BCE. Each of these cities had a god or goddess who regarded the site as their home. The moon god Nannar resided in Ur; the goddess of love and war, Ishtar, and the sky god, Anu, lived in Uruk; and at Eridu, the primeval city, the god Ea had his home.

The fertile soil and the technological innovations made by the people of southern Mesopotamia allowed large populations to survive in cities like Eridu for centuries. As hard as it may be to imagine given the weathered landscape seen there today, this was the original area of the "Garden of Eden". What the Bible calls Paradise, "Eden", was simply the Sumerian word *edin*, meaning the wild grassland of the south – the natural landscape that existed before the development of cities.[10]

While the regular floods made the land capable of growth, their timing presented a key difficulty. As the snow from the Anatolian highlands melted in the early spring, it caused the banks of the Tigris and Euphrates to release their floodwaters just as the crops on their banks were ripening. Left to its own devices, this would wash away all of the young shoots before they could mature and be harvested. Therefore, farmers would construct dams and levees to control where the floodwater went. Needless to say, this must have been a difficult task, and if a mistake was made it could spell disaster for entire fields of crops.[11] Later in the year, with the water level in the river at its lowest during the summer and fall, the fresh seeds could only be sown in November and December when there was a little rainfall.[12] The harvest generally took place between April and May.

Eridu was built at the conjunction of the western desert, the alluvial plain, and the marshes, the three main domains for people in Mesopotamia at that time. Nomadic pastoralism, fishing, and farming were the dominant ways of life, and the major plants that were irrigated were barley, wheat, millet, sesame, and pulses, such as lentils, beans, and peas. In addition, some of the crops that were likely grown in the gardens within and near Eridu include dates, onions, cucumbers, vines, figs, and apples.[13] The abrasive grit-rich bread that the people made meant that few of them would have reached old age with their teeth intact.

---

[9] Hall, H. R. (1923) "Ur and Eridu: the British Museum excavations of 1919." *The Journal of Egyptian Archaeology*, 9 (3/4), 177 - 195

[10] Millard, A. R. (1984) "The Etymology of Eden." *Vetus Testamentum*, 34, 103 - 106.

[11] It was only in the 1970s with the construction of the Hemrin Dam on the Diyala River – a tributary of the Tigris – that the waters could be reliably controlled.

[12] Crawford, 2004

[13] Adams, R. (1980) *Heartland of Cities: Surveys of Ancient Settlement and Land Use On the Central Floodplain at the Euphrates.*

Money did not exist in ancient Eridu, and an explanation for this can be found in the Eridu Genesis text found at Ur, which described the "bushel baskets" that were allotted to the first cities. Such baskets indicate a system of payment or remuneration that was based on the distribution of grain, not cash.[14] They also raised zebus, known as "humped cattle", and pigs.

In addition to grains, the people of Eridu would have eaten fish and river shellfish from the Euphrates and the southern marshes.[15] An abundance of fish bones have been found within the temple, showing signs of having been eaten and burnt. These were alongside strange, buried coiled snake-like objects, which hint towards ritual meals.[16] Herds of sheep were allowed to graze on the fields of young barley shoots – in return providing manure that made the land even more fertile.

The Persian Gulf used to extend about 30 miles further to the northwest than it currently does today, but even despite this, it is unlikely that Eridu ever stood anywhere close to the Persian Gulf. There is no evidence of aquatic faunal remains typically seen at archaeological sites that once existed on the sea shores, nor is there any geological indication that the gulf reached Eridu. However, there is evidence that Eridu was situated next to a large, marshy lake – perhaps connected to the foundation myths associated with the site.[17] The settlement may have been situated on a waterway that led from this lake to the gulf that has since dried up.

Thousands of years ago, the region bordering the Persian Gulf would have been quite dry despite the high water table, and the Ubaid people instituted a complex system of canals to harness the life-giving waters of the Tigris and the Euphrates, diverting it to irrigate their crops. As well as making agriculture more difficult, the aridity of southern Iraq also prevented the region from being well-forested, and since there was no sufficient supply of timber, it was not frequently used for the construction of buildings. People naturally opted to make use of the most prevalent resources in the area, much as the people of southern Iraq continue to do in the present day: reeds and mud. Generally, these marsh reeds were quite sturdy and could grow to a length of over 12 feet. The Ubaid people became adept at using reeds for a variety of purposes, constructing their dwellings and even entire floating villages out of them.

The earliest evidence of watercrafts in Mesopotamia came from the Ubaid period. Reed boats were the most common type of vessel used on southern Iraq's waterways, and bitumen was important in the construction of these crafts. This is a naturally occurring substance similar in appearance and properties to modern asphalt; it is black and oily, but it is also viscous and tar-

---

[14] Jacobsen, 1981
[15] Oates, 1960
[16] Safar, 'Ali Muṣṭafa, and Lloyd, 1981
[17] Hall, 1923

like. Therefore, it makes for an excellent sealant, and it was used by the Ubaids to make their boats and houses waterproof. They had originally used mud to seal their constructions, but it was a poor sealant that had to be constantly reapplied as it broke down. On the other hand, bitumen was impervious to moisture, and it was for the most part maintenance-free after its application.

Historians know that bitumen became an important part of the Ubaid people's societal growth thanks to a boat model that was found in As-Sabiyah, an archaeological site in modern-day Kuwait.[18] At this site, archaeologists discovered traces of a settlement that was tied to the Ubaid people based on the distinctive pottery found there. The small, ceramic boat model found there is indicative of the fact that the earliest Mesopotamian settlers used crafts like this, and the raised prow and stern of the boat are evidence that this was a model of a reed boat since this was typically where the ends of the reeds were tied together and bent.

Other artifacts discovered at As-Sabiyah provide further insight into the Ubaid people's boat construction. These include a number of bitumen chunks, many of which bear reed impressions on one side and barnacles on the other. Since the pottery at As-Sabiyah does not show signs of having been submerged in water, the only logical explanation for the presence of barnacles on the bitumen is that a reed structure was covered in the substance, and then submerged in the sea for an extended length of time. This suggests that even before the Sumerian cities began to grow in earnest, the Ubaid people had begun to trade with the fishing communities that lined the central Persian Gulf.

The Mythological City of Eridu

Looking at the earliest examples of writing in Mesopotamia, there is a place known as the "first city", the site where kingship and the notion of living in an urban setting – two things inextricably connected to what the Mesopotamians thought of civilization – were first given to humans by the gods. Eridu was the ancient city that started civilization in Mesopotamia, at least according to a rich and detailed mythological tradition that survived by being passed down through later written sources. The site is generally placed within a larger sequence of events, a narrative that describes the processes by which humanity was created, civilization emerged and the first cities were established.

Unlike other ancient urban sites in southern Mesopotamia, no inscribed tablets – whole or fragmented – have been discovered at Eridu. A small fragment of an inscribed alabaster mace head was discovered in 1918, dating to the 24th or 23rd centuries BCE,[19] and a few inscribed

---

[18] Carter, R. (2002) "Ubaid-period boat remains from As-Sabiyah: excavations by the British Archaeological Expedition to Kuwait." In *Proceedings of the Seminar for Arabian Studies*. Brepols.
[19] Hall, 1923

bricks have been found at the wall of the ziggurat restored by Bur Sin I (1831–1811 BCE), king of the city-state of Isin.[20] There are no examples of writing present at the site dating from later than the 3rd millennium BCE; for these, one has to look at the material discovered at other sites in the region. The Sumerian language became widely spoken during the end of the Uruk Period (though many other languages were also found amongst the diverse populations of the region). It was during this time that the earliest written records were produced, and it was also during this time that individual identities can be discerned in the textual and archaeological record.

The Sumerian King List is an ancient list of rulers of southern Mesopotamia dating back to around 2000 BCE that was written in the cuneiform script and discovered in fragmented forms at a number of sites throughout the region. It has served as the primary framework through which Mesopotamian chronologies have been identified by modern scholars because it provides a list of the ancient kings of Sumer, the length and location of their reign, and an unparalleled perspective into how contemporary Mesopotamians viewed their own history.[21] However, some stories push Eridu's foundation back even further than the quasi-chronology of the Sumerian King List. For example, a clay tablet fragment was discovered in Nippur during the excavations conducted there by Thorkild Jacobsen of the University of Chicago in the 1890s[22] and dated to the Old Babylonian period (around the 1600 BCE). This was the story known today as the "Eridu Genesis," and it reads, "All the lands were sea. The spring in the sea was a water pipe. Then Eridu was made, Esagila[23] was built, Esagila whose foundations Lugaldukuga laid within the Apsu... The gods, the Annunnaki he created equal. The holy city, the dwelling of their hearts' delight, they call it solemnly. Marduk constructed a reed frame on the face of the waters. He created dirt and poured it out by the reed frame. In order to settle the gods in the dwelling of [their] hearts' delight, he created mankind."[24]

The Eridu Genesis tale was likely recorded in written form for the first time around 1600 BCE, but it was probably orally transmitted between generations for a much longer period beforehand. As well as the Nippur tablet, another similar fragment was discovered in the city of Ur dating to roughly the same period, and a third bilingual example was discovered in Ashurbanipal's library of texts discovered in Nineveh and dated to the 7th century BCE. The various sources describe the same general series of events, albeit represented in their own fashion.

According to this narrative, Eridu was the first piece of creation separated out of the chaos that previously filled the universe. It is thus described as the place where the gods first came down to

---

[20] Hall, 1923
[21] Young, D. W. (1991) "The Incredible Regnal Spans of Kish I in the Sumerian King List." *Journal of Near Eastern Studies*, 50: 1. 23 – 35
[22] Though it was not dated or translated until much later; see Jacobsen, 1981
[23] Esagila was the primary religious site within Babylon associated with the home Babylonian god Marduk
[24] Leick, G. (2002) *Mesopotamia: The invention of the city*. Penguin UK.

live on Earth, and as the place associated with the creation of mankind before the Deluge.[25] It differs from the Sumerian King List, though the two were frequently amalgamated throughout later history. Like the King List, the Eridu Genesis narrative describes the sequence of early rulers in ancient Eridu and other cities; but the Eridu Genesis tale also provides a much richer account of the motives and actions of the gods, the symbiotic relationship between nature and culture, the foundation of the first cities and their rulers, and the predecessor to the flood myth popularly known today through the Book of Genesis in the Bible.

One of the primary sections of the Eridu Genesis narrative was the creation of not only mankind but all life on Earth. Unfortunately, the Ur text is fragmented, and the reasons for the creation of life remain unclear through this source alone. According to the parts that can be deciphered:

> "When An, Enlil, Enki, and Ninhursaga
> fashioned the dark-headed (people)
> they had made the small animals (that come up) from (out of) the earth
> come from the earth in abundance
> and had let there be, as befits (it), gazelles,
> (wild) donkeys, and four-footed beasts in the desert."

The Ur text illustrates some of the preexisting conditions of mankind in between their creation and the foundation of the first cities. The tablet mentions the lack of waterworks in the ancient times, and by extension an absence of irrigation in the land. Even pastoralism was not yet being practiced; according to the text, the deity Sumukan, god of herding, had not yet appeared on Earth.[26] Since they had no animals from which to get leather, the ancients are described as going about naked. Humans were created out of clay, and how well they were crafted and baked determined their lot in life. There were well-baked princes, badly baked peasants, and everything in between.[27]

Given this context, a key feature in the narrative is the process by which nomadic peoples became sedentary. This was primarily driven by the Sumerian mother goddess Ninhursag, and it was described as being a service to the gods: "May they come and build cities and cult-places, that I may cool myself in their shade; may they lay the bricks for the cult-cities in pure spots, and may they found places for divination in pure spots!"[28]

---

[25] Jacobsen, T. (1981) "The Eridu Genesis." *Journal of Biblical Literature, 100* (4), 513 - 529.
[26] Jacobsen, 1981
[27] Jacobsen, 1981
[28] Jacobsen, 1981

Therefore, the city itself was a sacred concept, a gift of the gods and a place of stability against the chaos of nature, but with the condition that the residents of the city were expected to serve the gods by working in their temples. It is notable that the first building described in the Nippur tablet is a temple, reinforcing the idea that the primary function of the city was sacred – a place to gather people together in service of the divine. In fact, the quarter of Babylon that contained Esagila was also called "Eridu", harking back to the sacred place where the gift of civilization was first passed from god to man.[29]

One of the most interesting passages of the Eridu Genesis narrative comes from the tablet discovered at Ur. It describes the adoption of kingship by the ancients, and as a result the organization of labor which produced irrigation:

> "When the royal sceptre was coming down from heaven,
> the august crown and the royal throne being already down from heaven,
> he (the king) regularly performed to perfection
> the august divine services and offices,
> laid the bricks of those cities in pure spots.
> They were named by name and allotted half-bushel baskets.
>
> "The firstling of those cities, Eridu,
> she gave to the leader Nudimmud[30],
> the second, Badtibira, she gave to the Prince and Sacred One
> the third, Larak, she gave to Pabilsag,
> the fourth, Sippar, she gave to the gallant, Utu.
> the fifth, Shuruppak, she gave to Sud.
>
> "These cities, which had been named by names,
> and been allotted half-bushel baskets,
> dredged the canals, which were blocked with purplish
> (wind-borne) clay, and they carried water.
> Their cleaning of the smaller canals
> established abundant growth."[31]

The Sumerian King List provides a list of the first kings that ruled over the city of Eridu. It states, "After the kingship descended from heaven, the kingship was in Eridu. In Eridu, Alulim became king; he ruled for 28,800 years. Alaljar ruled for 36,000 years. 2 kings; they ruled for

---

[29] Montet, E. (1909) "Israel and Babylonian Civilization." *The Open Court, 1909* (10), 4.
[30] Another name for Enki, specifically referring to his role as a god of creation.
[31] Jacobsen, 1981

64,800 years. Then Eridu fell and the kingship was taken to Bad-tibira. In Bad-tibira, En-men-lu-ana ruled for 43,200 years. En-men-gal-ana ruled for 28,800 years. Dumuzid, the shepherd, ruled for 36,000 years. 3 kings; they ruled for 108,000 years. Then Bad-tibira fell and the kingship was taken to Larag. In Larag, En-sipad-zid-ana ruled for 28,800 years. 1 king; he ruled for 28,800 years. Then Larag fell and the kingship was taken to Zimbir. In Zimbir, En-men-dur-ana became king; he ruled for 21,000 years. 1 king; he ruled for 21,000 years. Then Zimbir fell and the kingship was taken to Curuppag. In Curuppag, Ubara-Tutu became king; he ruled for 18,600 years. 1 king; he ruled for 18,600 years. In 5 cities 8 kings; they ruled for 241,200 years. Then the flood swept over."[32]

The King List has several points of interest. The kings all have enormously inflated reigns, similar to those of the descendants of Adam in the Bible and the Greek mythological Golden Age of Man. It provides the idea that this first city, Eridu, existed before the Flood in an age when gods walked with mankind on Earth. In fact, the first person on the King List known to have existed through archaeological evidence is Enmebaragesi, who reigned over Kish (present day Tell al-Uhaymir, near Babylon) around 2600 BCE.[33]

The King List is, in many ways, an attempt to trace contemporary Sumerian civilization all the way back to Heaven, giving heritage and legitimacy to these people, much the same way Julius Caesar tried to claim that he was descended from the god Venus. The King List also gives the idea that kingship and civilization do not have to reside in one specific place but can instead be passed down through and between cities, similar to the Chinese Mandate of Heaven, which passed from one dynasty to the next as each lost the support of the gods.

The Eridu Genesis discovered in Ashurbanipal's library at Nineveh provides another version of this chronology. Like the Sumerian King List, the Eridu Genesis tablet from Nineveh describes the reign of each king in grossly exaggerated terms, ranging from at least 10,800 years to 64,800 years.[34] According to the tablet, the earliest kings at Eridu were Alulim, whose reign lasted for 36,000 years; Alagar, whose reign lasted for 10,800 years; and then two unnamed kings who ruled for 46,800 years.[35] The list continued with the reigns of the kings of Bad-tibira, Sippar, Larak, and Shuruppak. It ended by describing Enlil's eventual displeasure with mankind, and it seems to be for an awfully strange reason: their noisiness kept him awake whenever he tried to sleep![36] This disquiet had severe repercussions for mankind, leading to their almost complete destruction in the Deluge that covered the Earth.

---

[32] Kramer, S. N. (1983) "The Sumerian Deluge Myth." *Anatolian Studies, 33*, 115 - 121.
[33] Charvat, P. (1976) "The oldest royal dynasty of ancient Mesopotamia." *Archív Orientální, 44*, 346-352.
[34] Jacobsen, 1981
[35] Jacobsen, 1981
[36] Jacobsen, 1981

The four deities frequently mentioned in the Eridu Genesis were amongst the most important worshipped in ancient Mesopotamia. These were An, Ninhursag, Enlil, and Enki. An was the Sumerian sky goddess, known by the Akkadians and Babylonians as the goddess Antu. Ninhursag was the Sumerian mother goddess, a deity associated with fertility and mountains. Enlil was one of the chief deities of the Sumerian pantheon, the god of wind associated with the city of Nippur.[37]

A detail depicting Enki on an ancient seal

Eridu is primarily associated with the god Enki, who is also called Ea in Akkadian and Babylonian, of whom there are many myths. One was the myth of Adapa, the mortal son of Enki, who was a priest at Eridu. The Adapa myth portrays Adapa as the ruler and priest of Eridu, preparing the bread, collecting water for the city, and hunting for its food. Adapa also appears in

---

[37] Ristvet, L. (2014) *Ritual, Performance, and Politics in the Ancient Near East*. Cambridge: Cambridge University Press.

later writing as Oannes, a half-man, half-fish demigod who was one of the Apkallu, the Seven Sages that taught the wisdom of civilization to mankind. One of the earliest tablets of this myth reads:

> "He [Adapa] possessed intelligence...
> His command like the command of Anu...
> He [the god Ea] granted him a wide ear to reveal the destiny of the land,
> He granted him wisdom, but he did not grant him eternal life.
> In those days, in those years the wise man of Eridu,
> Ea had created him as chief among men,
> A wise man whose command none should oppose,
> The prudent, the most wise among the Anunnaki was he,
> Blameless, of clean hands, anointed, observer of the divine statutes,
> With the bakers he made bread
> With the bakers of Eridu, he made bread,
> The food and the water for Eridu he made daily,
> With his clean hands he prepared the table,
> And without him the table was not cleared.
> The ship he steered, fishing and hunting for Eridu he did.
> Then Adapa of Eridu
> While Ea, in the chamber, upon the bed.
> Daily the closing of Eridu he attended to.
> Upon the pure dam, the new moon dam) he embarked upon the ship,
> The wind blew and his ship departed,
> With the oar, be steered his ship Upon the broad sea..."[38]

As he was out fishing one day a gust of wind overturned his boat, and in revenge he broke the wings of Ninlil, the goddess of the South Wind.[39] This angered the gods, and he was called to Heaven to answer for his actions. His father, Enki, warned him not to eat the food and drink that was put before him in Heaven, warning Adapa that it would kill him. However, in reality the food of the gods would have granted immortality to Adapa, so by refusing the food, Adapa returned to Earth a mortal man. Some have thought that Enki intentionally tricked his son so that he would never be on par, or threaten, his position in the heavens. Thus, humanity was kept in its rightful mortal place. Soon after his return to earth Adapa suddenly disappeared into the sea, but six other sages like him appeared and dwelled in Eridu, teaching human initiates the wisdom and science that had been lost in the flood.[40]

---

[38] Rogers, R. W. (1912) *Cuneiform parallels to the Old Testament.* Eaton and Mains.
[39] Langdon, S. (1923) "Two Sumerian Hymns from Eridu and Nippur." *The American Journal of Semitic Languages and Literatures, 39* (3), 161 - 186.
[40] Green, M. W. (1975) *Eridu in Sumerian Literature.* Chicago: University of Chicago

As that myth indicates, Enki was an interesting character in his own right, and though he was called Ea in Akkad and Babylon, the two deities have slightly different histories. Further north in Akkad, he was identified as Ea, worshiped as a more serious water god (the position of which he won in a dice game), and is also depicted as half-fish and half-human. In Eridu, Enki was a trickster god, lord of water and husband of Ninhursag. Enki built Eridu and filled it with metaphorical treasures, such as "happiness", "honor", and "kissing".[41]

Sumerian myths also tell how the arts of civilization that originated here in Eridu would bring both joy and sorrow. They believed that this was what the gods passed on from here to future ages. The divine couple lived together in Paradise, where Enki reportedly enjoyed sex, and it was with Ninhursag that the world was born with his "fresh water" (the Sumerian description of semen, and water was therefore associated with Enki's sperm).[42] Eridu is described in the Sippar tablet as a settlement built upon a reed mat floating on a great sea of fresh water stretching away to the south – the primeval waters known as the Abzu – much as the Arabs living on the marshlands of southern Iraq still construct their dwellings in the present day.

The Great Flood

The Bible's tale of Noah and the Ark was not the only ancient source to describe a flood that covered the world and swept away a corrupt mankind. Amongst the earliest versions of the Deluge narrative were those that came from Eridu, or were otherwise associated with its role in the creation of mankind and civilization.[43] As the Nineveh tablet mentioned, the god Enlil was fed up with the noise and ruckus produced by humans. According to the text, the last antediluvian king, Ziusudra, was in his capital at Shuruppak[44] when he was warned by Enki in a dream of what was about to come:

> "And as Ziusudra stood there beside it he went on hearing:
> 'Step up to the wall to my left and listen!
> Let me speak a word to you at the wall
> and may you grasp what I say,
> May you heed my advice!
> By our hand a flood will sweep over
> (the cities of) the half-bushelbaskets, and the country,
> the decision, that mankind is to be destroyed, has been made,
> a verdict, a command by the assembly,

---

[41] Langdon, 1923
[42] Kramer, S. N., and Albright, W. F. (1945) "Enki and Ninḫursag: A Sumerian" Paradise" Myth." *Bulletin of the American Schools of Oriental Research. Supplementary Studies*, (1), 1 - 40
[43] Green, M. W. (1975) *Eridu in Sumerian Literature*. Chicago: University of Chicago
[44] Present day Tell Fara, approximately 35 miles north of Nippur

> cannot be revoked,
> an order of An and Enlil is not known
> ever to have been countermanded..."[45]

Ziusudra responded by building a boat, though it is unclear if this was his idea or suggested to him by Enki. It is also unclear how the boat was built, since that section of the Nineveh tablet is missing. Where the text reappears next, the Deluge had already started:

> "All evil winds, all stormy winds gathered into one
> and with them, the Flood was sweeping over (the cities of)
> the half-bushel baskets
> for seven days and seven nights.
> After the flood had swept over the country,
> after the evil wind had tossed the big boat
> about on the great waters,
> the sun came out spreading light
> over heaven and earth.
> Ziusudra then drilled an opening in the big boat.
> and the gallant Utu[46] sent
> his light into the interior of the big boat.
> Ziusudra, being a king,
> stepped up before Utu kissing the ground (before him)."[47]

Enlil was the perpetrator of the Deluge, but thanks to the intervention of Enki, humanity was saved, and Enki eventually managed to convince the gods to put an end to the flood. They felt some degree of remorse over their actions and were therefore delighted upon discovering that some humans had been saved:

> "Ziusudra, being king, stepped up before An and Enlil
> kissing the ground,
> And An and Enlil did well by him,
> were granting him life like a god's,
> were making lasting breath of life, like a god's
> descend into him.
> That day they made Ziusudra,

---

[45] Jacobsen, 1981
[46] The sun god
[47] Jacobsen, 1981

> preserver as king of the name of the small
> animals and the seed of mankind,
> live toward the east over the mountains
> in Mount Tilmun."[48]

The relationship between the Eridu Genesis myth and the Biblical Genesis narrative has been explored by many scholars.[49] Both describe the creation of mankind and animals; both provide a list of important individuals after the Creation; and both describe the Flood. The story of the Eridu Genesis is relatively optimistic and progressive in tone.[50] Whereas in the Bible things started out perfect but the Flood occurred as a result of mankind's sinfulness and worsening conditions on Earth, in the Eridu Genesis things were not ideal to begin with, and while the flood occurred in order to remove this blight, it resulted in providing a stage for mankind's progression.

Linking Myth to History

Given the many fanciful myths about Eridu, it surprised many people to find that the city was in fact a real place after it was discovered by archaeologists in the mid-19th century. In the wake of World War I, the region came under British control with the name "State of Iraq," and the British Museum organized a number of archaeological expeditions to Mesopotamia. Their role was not only to protect the heritage of the region but also acquire objects to be brought back to London for exhibition.

Several important archaeological studies have been conducted at Eridu. The first took place during the time of the Crimean War (1853–1856). One of the first Europeans to explore the archaeology of the region was William Kennett Loftus, a British geologist and archaeologist and a member of the Turco-Persian Frontier Commission, through which he had the opportunity to visit archaeological sites in the region. He later returned to the region on an expedition organized by the Assyrian Excavation Fund in 1853, but he never actually excavated at Eridu.[51] Instead, it was an associate of his, the British Vice Consul at Basrah named John George Taylor, who first went to the site in 1854.[52] The site was also visited by Ernest Wallis Budge in 1888, but the ruling Turkish authorities at the time refused to let him stay for very long.[53]

---

[48] Jacobsen, 1981
[49] See for example Davila, J. R. (1995) "The flood hero as king and priest." *Journal of Near Eastern Studies*, 54 (3), 199 - 214.
[50] Jacobsen, 1981
[51] Hall, 1923
[52] Taylor, J. E. (1855) "Notes on Abu Shahrein and Tel el Lahm." *The Journal of the Royal Asiatic Society of Great Britain and Ireland*, 15, 404-415.
[53] Hall, 1923

Loftus

Budge

Thus, the first actual excavations were carried out in 1918 by the British archaeologist Captain Reginald Campbell Thompson of the British Museum in London.[54] Thompson was then serving as captain of the Intelligence branch of the British army. His excavations at Eridu became the most authoritative study of the site since the survey conducted by Taylor; with the pits that he dug into the mound he became the first to reveal the complex stratigraphy of the site.

Excavations continued under the renowned Egyptologist Henry Reginald Holland Hall in 1919, and he focused on the standing structural remains of the site, especially in the southern side.[55] He excavated five residential complexes along a street. Despite the difficulties caused by the rapidly shifting sands that covered the site, which would fill up the trenches as soon as they had been excavated, he managed to excavate a large amount of the site. He also explored the large, stone bastions of the site. Being so rare in the region, the presence of tremendous stone structures at Eridu was remarkable.

---

[54] Hall, H. R. (2014). *A Season's Work at Ur, Al-'Ubaid, Abu Shahrain-Eridu-and Elsewhere: Being an Unofficial Account of the British Museum Archaeological Mission to Babylonia, 1919.* Routledge.
[55] Hall, 1923

Ultimately, in light of the spectacular finds discovered at Nineveh at about the same time, the archaeologists at Eridu thought that there was little fit to grace the European museums. Therefore, the investigations at the site were minimal, at least in comparison to other contemporary projects in the region. It was not until the expedition of 1946-1949 that the mound of Abu Shahrain was excavated by Seton Lloyd and Fuad Safar.[56] Lloyd and Safar were working on behalf of the newly-independent state of Iraq, the first modern independent Mesopotamian state, and the symbolism of this project is clear to see, with the new secular state affirming its historical and pre-Islamic foundations by laying claim to its rich ancient heritage, the heritage of Eridu and Mesopotamia. These motives are, in many ways, quite similar to the motives of those that compiled the Sumerian King List; both sought to trace their origins back into prehistory.

Lloyd and Safar found a mound dominated by the remains of a great stepped ziggurat with inscribed bricks that named Amar Sin of the Third Dynasty of Ur (ca. 2047 – 2039 BCE) as its builder. Digging beneath the corner of the great ziggurat, they found the remains of earlier temples, and they discovered evidence of more than 18 levels of occupation on the site – a staggering depth, both tangibly and temporally. Over time, the layers were divided into four periods based on the ceramics found within, with two main periods of occupation identified at Eridu; first came the 'Ubaid town and temple mound of the 7th millennium, with a Third Dynasty of Ur ziggurat sacred landscape superimposed upon the mound in the 3rd millennium.[57]

The main mound of Eridu is roughly circular in shape, and is approximately 1750 feet x 1700 feet in size. While mud brick structures such as those built at Eridu were in a sense permanent, they also required constant maintenance, and mounds like these were built up over millennia with the accumulated debris of human settlements being torn down and replaced every couple of generations. The surrounding urban area was taken up by the homes of its population, but most of the monumental structures at Eridu were focused in the temple precinct, which was centered on this mound. These buildings evolved and changed over time. At the earliest layers the temple consisted of nothing more than a simple single-roomed structure built upon the sand, but it eventually grew into a massive religious complex. The site was occasionally leveled off and filled with sand and soil in order to create a firm foundation for the next stage of building. This amount of brick architecture at the southern Ubaid site was unusual, indicating Eridu was something special.

As a result, the temples at Eridu were built directly on top of each other over the centuries, becoming steadily larger and grander in each period. The buildings were up to 7 feet high and

---

[56] Safar, F., 'Ali Muṣṭafa, M., and Lloyd, S. (1981) *Eridu*. Republic of Iraq, Ministry of Culture and Information, State Organization of Antiquites and Heritage.
[57] Taylor, J. E. (1855) "Notes on Abu Shahrein and Tel el Lahm." *The Journal of the Royal Asiatic Society of Great Britain and Ireland*, 15, 404 - 415

made of rectangular mud bricks. Some of the walls were faced with a hard, white stucco plaster and were also occasionally painted with alternating stripes of red and white.[58] They were spacious, with large niches and traces of what may have been windows. Any timber elements of the structures have completely disappeared over time, but the discovery of copper nails indicates that the material would have been used in some manner.[59]

The upper levels explored showed Ubaid and Late Ubaid remains dated to around 3800 BCE, and below this was a layer that contained Choga Mami ceramics, named after a small Tell site near Uruk and dated to around 4700-4600 BCE.[60] The Choga Mami is thought to have been a bridging link between the earlier styles and the widespread use of Ubaid culture. At the bottom was the earliest ceramic remains of a type dubbed "Eridu ware" or Ubaid I, thought to date to around 4900 BCE.[61]

The site appears to have grown to its greatest extent during the 'Ubaid period (5400–4700 BCE). The temple built during this time was almost 75 feet long. It had formidable mudbrick walls supported by buttresses.[62] During the Uruk period (ca. 4000–3100 BCE) the temple mound was surrounded by a temenos measuring approximately 600 square feet, enclosed by a retaining wall to form a massive temple platform. A number of additional buildings were erected in this sacred precinct, and a tripartite temple structure was built. This tripartite structure is one of the only standard temple plans that have been identified in the Uruk period, being found also at Eanna.[63] It consisted of a rectangular central hall with smaller rooms constructed along its walls. An altar was positioned against the shorter wall, and a hearth for offerings was positioned in the center of the space. The Uruk temple platform was used as the foundation for the ziggurat that was erected at the site by the Third Dynasty kings of Ur, and that would later became the quintessential religious structure throughout Mesopotamia.[64] In the early Uruk period Eridu is estimated to have had a total area of 40-45 hectares, but by the Early Dynastic Period (2900 – 2350 BCE) the city had spread across seven mounds.

In the Jemdat Nasr and Early Dynastic I periods, a number of large public buildings appear at sites throughout southern Mesopotamia, linked by their architectural style, but it remains unclear what their functions were or if they shared the same function. They have been frequently described as "palaces," yet there is no evidence of Eridu serving as a seat for any secular dynastic power in southern Mesopotamia during this time. Regardless, the structures consisted of

---

[58] Hall, 1923
[59] Hall, 1923
[60] Oates, J. (1969) "Choga Mami, 1967–68: A preliminary report." *Iraq, 31* (02), 115 - 152.
[61] Oates, J. (1960) "Ur and Eridu, the prehistory." *Iraq, 22* (1-2), 32 - 50.
[62] Simons, 1994
[63] Crawford, 2004
[64] Lloyd, 1960

a buttressed external wall surrounding a great number of small internal chambers interconnected by narrow corridors. They may have been multi-storied buildings, based on the sheer thickness of the remains of the walls and the presence of architectural elements that may have been staircases (though these may have simply led to the flat roof).[65]

Archaeological evidence indicates that the floor plans of the non-temple structures of Eridu display a notable similarity with the temple architecture of the city. A number of monumental households existed in close proximity to the temple complex, and two of these have been excavated.[66] The first consisted of a rectangular central courtyard (or hall), nearly 40 feet by 6 feet in size, with doorways leading to smaller rooms on both of the longer sides. Entrance was through the short wall to the southwest. Within one of the rooms was a kiln constructed atop a brick platform, and there is evidence that it was used to melt bitumen.[67] Although the extent of their decoration is relatively unknown, evidence of a rose-colored plaster was found in the ruins, and the structure has been interpreted as being the residence of an important priest.[68] A second building consisted of three main rooms in which a number of artefacts had been deposited, perhaps as votive offerings.

The mixing of deep tradition with innovation was therefore a key part of Mesopotamian culture. Many developments of civilization occurred during the Ubaid period, including the coming together of large groups of people and the construction of more permanent structures. Stone was rare in southern Mesopotamia, and therefore it was fired mud bricks that were primarily used for the construction of buildings at Eridu. The temples at Eridu were built using these mud bricks with a clay mortar, and while the ziggurats that were to become so iconic in Mesopotamia were not yet evident during the Ubaid period, the increasingly large platforms upon which the temples were constructed foreshadowed this later development.

Ceramic Production

Ceramic styles changed more frequently than the city's architecture. Because of their abundance and evolution, early Mesopotamian history is split into chronological periods associated with human cultures that are defined according to the pottery that they produced. While Eridu is described as the "first city", in truth it grew from what came before. The Ubaid period and culture was the setting for Eridu as a living city. Having peacefully taken over the Halaf culture (ca. 6100–5100 BCE) in the north, the Ubaid emerged from the mists of prehistory around 6000 BCE in the south, and it ended in approximately 4000 BCE with the onset of the

---

[65] Margueron, J. C. (1985) Archéologie mésopotamienne. *École pratique des hautes études. 4e section, sciences historiques et philologiques. Livret, 114* (2), 40 - 41.
[66] Safar, 'Ali Muṣṭafa, and Lloyd, 1981
[67] Safar, 'Ali Muṣṭafa, and Lloyd, 1981
[68] Crawford, 2004

Uruk period.

It was during the Halaf-Ubaid Transitional period between 5500 and 5200 BCE that the first true villages of mudbrick structures began to appear in Sumer. Their inhabitants fished on the Persian Gulf and cultivated crops on the alluvium spread by the flooding rivers. It was from these villages that the city of Eridu grew. While it possessed Ubaid wares, it also showed evidence in its deepest levels of a previously unknown pottery of a pre-Ubaid type, seen nowhere else apart from Ur and a site named Usaila close to Eridu.[69] This pushed the shared Ubaid culture, of which Eridu is associated, even further back in time. There were likely even earlier periods of occupation, but no material remains of these have been found; the site was likely used by semi-nomadic groups on a temporary basis.

Eridu was an Ubaid town and is one of the key sources of knowledge about the Ubaid culture. Eridu has revealed some of the finest examples of 'Ubaid ceramics, though Al 'Ubaid is the type site from which the culture received its name. Approximately 3 miles further north and west of Ur is the site of Al 'Ubaid, where the remains of a large and well-preserved temple complex have been discovered on the tell-mound, and where a large scatter of distinctive ceramic sherds was found of a type known today as 'Ubaid ware.

Whereas a great quantity of 'Ubaid ceramics have been discovered at archaeological sites across southern Mesopotamia, it was not until relatively recent that their centers and processes of production have been understood. Evidence has been found of ceramics having been fired in two locations at Eridu: a large area close to the graveyard, and a smaller one close to the southeast corner of the temenos wall.[70] The former contained a very dense collection of ceramic sherds, indicating that this was the main firing site of the city, and the spot where vast quantities of pottery were produced. Moreover, due to the large amount of smoke produced by ceramic production, this location at the edge of the city would have been desirable; the craft activities could occur away from the residential and cult areas of the settlement, and the debris of the manufacturing process could easily be discarded from the edge of the mound.[71] The city seems to have been a major center for the production of these ceramics, the use of which spread across southern Mesopotamia.

The presence of pottery at Eridu's earliest levels shows that its original population was already familiar with the techniques of ceramic manufacture. Spouts and loop-handles make their first appearance in the ceramics found there, and during the Ubaid period statues of lizard-headed

---

[69] Oates, 1960
[70] Moore, 2002
[71] Moore, 2002

women and some male figures were also being produced there, as were sling pellets, weights, and even clay sickles.[72] The pottery of the Ubaid is thought to be especially beautiful, consisting of thin, delicate walls decorated of dots, dashes, geometric patterns, and even animal and human figures.[73] These were not roughly made all-purpose storage items suitable for a nomadic lifestyle but items of beauty, likely for an elite group and therefore evidence of a stratified social structure emerging in this time. They required specialized skills to manufacture, and it was the manufacture and storage of these ceramics that was potentially a contributing factor to the rise of sedentary society.

Gradually, the earlier styles of pottery were replaced by a style that was distinctly monochrome in decoration, consisting mainly of burnished grey dishes with molded rims. These are known as beveled-rim bowls – the so-called Uruk ware.[74] While the form of these dishes was far more sophisticated than that which came before, their decorative scheme was relatively bland. Of course, the pottery was not purely aesthetic; it was evidently used in large communal meals, which must have helped foster a sense of unity amongst those who shared in them. It may have also lent prestige and authority to those who were able to organize meals of this size.

Religion

During the earliest periods of urbanization in southern Mesopotamia a select number of urban sites were singled out as major economic or administrative centers. Of these, one of the largest and most important was Ur. But religious centers also grew to become equally great in size and reputation, and of these there was no rival to the shrine of Enki at Eridu.

What exactly were the consequences, if not benefits, of civilization and the creation of cities according to the ancient sources? According to the tablet from Ur, they included the adoption of kingship and proper leadership,[75] but cities also provided an avenue by which mankind to collectively worship the gods, and based on the ancient myths surrounding Eridu, the organization of society under a leading priest was of foremost importance.

What was the role of the priest in ancient Eridu? Another link can be made with the Eridu Genesis text from Nineveh. In the section that described the warnings made by Enki to Ziusudra before the Deluge, it presented the human king as a prophet and priest. This was a particularly important aspect of kingship in ancient Sumer; the position of the king was something between being mortal and deified. He served as a middle-man, so to speak, of communication between

---

[72] Safar, 'Ali Muṣṭafa, and Lloyd, 1981
[73] Oates, 1960
[74] Lloyd, 1960
[75] Jacobsen, 1981

mankind and the gods. Furthermore, he served as a seer; through dreams and rites he was able to discern the wishes and warnings of the gods and steer his subjects down the correct path. Ziusudra himself was described as a *guda-abzu* ("libation priest") in the Nineveh text.[76]

The priests of Eridu may have held a number of administrative roles as well. They may have overseen agriculture, trade, and crafts that took place in the city; one of the key factors behind the growth of these earliest cities was the collective social organization that was required to maintain the irrigation systems required to survive in southern Mesopotamia. Archaeological evidence at the sites of Tell Al 'Ubaid and Eridu indicate that the production of 'Ubaid pottery occurred on a massive scale at these urban centers, a scale that could only have been done with the organization of a centralized bureaucratic power. This power may have been held by the priests.

At the heart of the city's activity was the temple, and Eridu was not unique in having its temple as its focal point. In fact, nearly all Sumerian cities appear to have grown not around palaces or fortresses but surrounding central temple sites. The city was a sacred landscape, and the people were drawn by the temple within as a liminal location between earthly life and the heavens. The people clearly valued the temple, and special attention seems to have been given to sealing off and preserving the plan of the central temple before a new structure was built, suggesting that they felt a sense of sacredness for the site and its heritage. At the same time, the amount of debris and food scraps that appear in the temple's archaeological remains make it clear that in the minds of the city's citizens, this site was not something separated from their lives – to be kept cold and immaculate like the Egyptian temples, which were the realm of the priests solely.[77]

The temple was built on a hill within a 65 foot depression called the Khor el Nejeif, or the "Abzu". This allowed water to collect in a seasonal lagoon, which still happens in the present day.[78] The city was associated with deities of sweet, drinkable water, a scarce and precious resource in the hot region. It is therefore clear to see how the temple and the body of water became joined together as a holy site. Because of its sturdy build as a brick structure in a world of reed huts and shifting waterways the site of Eridu would also have symbolized permanence; a site elevated beyond the chaos of nature. In Sumerian cosmology, the world was considered as a floating structure upon a body of water, so the sacred lagoon in the first city became enmeshed in its symbolism as a holy site. Eridu was in fact a map of the cosmos, of the structure of reality in miniature. By comparing it to sites like Göbekli Tepe in Anatolia, the building of sacred sites may have predated the development of agriculture.[79] This site, dating to the 10th millennium

---

[76] Burrows, E. (1932) "Problems of the abzu." *Orientalia, 1*, 231 - 256.
[77] Safar, 'Ali Muṣṭafa, and Lloyd, 1981
[78] Crawford, 2004
[79] Schmidt, K. (2010) "Göbekli Tepe–the Stone Age Sanctuaries. New results of ongoing excavations with a special

BCE, would have been almost as old to the inhabitants of Eridu as they themselves are to modern society. It may indicate that it was the lure of the temple and of the coming together for sacred purposes and ritual meals that fostered agriculture, not the other way around.

The great temple at Eridu – the most famous shrine in all of Sumer – was named after the Abzu. It was equated with the primeval ocean of sweet water, out of which all human and natural life came, so they believed. When archaeologists dug deep into the temple mound they discovered that around the time of 5000 BCE, a little sand mound surrounded by a reed fence once stood at the site of the temple. Upon the sandy hill was a tiny chapel marking the site of the mound of Creation.

Some of the small finds discovered at Eridu include small cones made of clay and red sandstone, ceramic sickles and nails, a peg of solid gold, a quartz pendant depicting a lion, and miniature ceramic figurines.[80] Between the 8th and 14th levels of the temple mound was discovered a number of flat vessels with flaring spouts described by archaeologists as "tortoise jars", which bear striking similarities to similar lenticular jars discovered at the site of Tepe Gawra.[81] A "fan" of flint and obsidian flakes was found to spread out on three sides of the main temple mound, especially to the south and southeast, indicating that this was a site for the production of stone tools in ancient times. It is likely that these washed down from the mound.

A moderately sized cemetery was located near the temple kiln site, containing two groups of burials in which both children and adults had been placed upon a bed of pot sherds in clay and brick-lined graves.[82] In similar graves, adult couples were frequently buried together. It yielded evidence of between 800 and 1000 bodies when it was discovered, of which around 200 have been excavated.[83] The cemetery contained ceramics from pre-'Ubaid periods, but there was also a remarkable appearance of new types of pottery and of a huge quantity of Uruk ceramics.[84] A jar, a wide dish, and a cup, along with jewelry, were left in these internments, but in the graves of the latest periods of occupation at Eridu no more than a single item was placed in each burial. Figurines of lizard-headed people in boats, along with special pottery such as miniatures for children, and food offerings found only in the cemetery, indicate that the people of Eridu must have observed funerary rites and likely held some belief about the afterlife. The burial of couples indicates that the people of Eridu practiced some form of monogamy, and the grave goods suggest that personal items were owned. Some dogs were also buried, perhaps as important or favored pets.

---

focus on sculptures and high reliefs." *Documenta Praehistorica, 37*, 239 - 256.
[80] Hall, 1923
[81] Woolley, L. (1981) *The development of Sumerian art*. Greenwood Press.
[82] Lloyd, 1960
[83] Crawford, 2004
[84] Oates, 1960

The Decline of Eridu

Eridu was not a city that existed in isolation but was rather part of a culture linked by the land, the rivers, and the sea. The ceramic style of the Late Ubaid period is found at sites south along the Persian Gulf, and at sites along the Syrian coast as well, demonstrating that Eridu was part of a culture that traded and extended itself far beyond the confines of the southern Tigris and Euphrates region. At several Ubaid sites obsidian and bitumen have been found, while gold and the Indian stone amazonite has been found at Ur.[85] These commodities cannot be found in Mesopotamia, and the fact that these precious resources found their way to its cities again suggests the people of Eridu were connected to the wider world.

Things were different in northern Mesopotamia. While they shared many similarities with their southern neighbors, the difference in local resources provided for a distinctive style.[86] Stones were easier to acquire, but reeds were not, leading to differences in temple architecture. The northerners also produced a great number of stone stamps seals, many with animal and human figures engraved on their surface, and they also buried their dead in a different manner, with the bodies interred on their sides and in groups surrounding individual houses, and with children buried in urns.[87] Much of this difference goes beyond mere geographical location; it can be attributed to the fact that the north had the distinctive Halaf culture prior to its adoption of the Ubaid way. Whether the eventual presence of Ubaid characteristics points to the migration of people from the south to the north or was simply spread by proximity cannot be said.

Relatively little is known about trade during the Uruk period, but archaeological evidence indicates that pack animals such as donkeys could have been used for overland trade as early as the Uruk period.[88] Cows may also have been used to draw wagons, the wheel having been in use from the end of the Ubaid period.[89] Sherds of vessels made of aragonite, also known as alabaster, suggest that trade may have taken place between Eridu and Egypt.[90] Copper was even more difficult to acquire, the closest sources being in Iran, Anatolia, and the Arabian Peninsula.[91] Cedar appears to have been used in particular in the temple buildings, and this would have been acquired overland from the mountains of Lebanon, the land of ancient Phoenicia. Keeping the

---

[85] Stein, G. (1994) "Economy, ritual, and power in 'Ubaid Mesopotamia." *Chiefdoms and early states in the Near East: the organizational dynamics of complexity, 18*, 35 - 46.
[86] Ur, J. A. (2010) "Cycles of civilization in northern Mesopotamia, 4400–2000 BC." *Journal of Archaeological Research, 18* (4), 381 - 431.
[87] Ur, 2010
[88] Way, K. C. (2010) "Assessing sacred asses: Bronze Age donkey burials in the Near East." *Levant, 42*(2), 210-225.
[89] Crawford, 2004
[90] Garner, H. (1956) "An early piece of glass from Eridu." *Iraq, 18* (02), 147 - 149.
[91] Edens, C. (1992) "Dynamics of trade in the ancient mesopotamian "World System"." *American Anthropologist, 94* (1), 118 - 139.

temple complex and other structures in the city in a good condition would have required regular trade with sources of lime and bitumen.[92]

Throughout its use, variations in the pottery found in Eridu are evolutionary, showing that the people who visited and lived there identified as one culture. The ziggurat built during the Third Dynasty of Ur at Eridu testifies to the cultural and religious significance of the city millennia after it was first settled, and millennia after it ceased to be a living city.[93] These indicate the continuity of the culture in which Eridu existed, at least in the minds of its people, for while Eridu ceased to be a functioning settlement at the beginning of the Uruk period (ca. 4000–3100 BCE), for centuries it remained a sanctuary with a temple still in use. In the later Uruk period, smaller settlements elsewhere in southern Mesopotamia began to expand – some almost doubling in size – while Eridu appears to have been abandoned.[94] At the same time, a great number of new settlements were founded in different sites, just as cities like Uruk reached their maximum size.[95] In the Early Dynastic III period (ca. 2500 – 2375 BCE) the city was reoccupied, with two so-called palace structures built in the vicinity of the temple mound.[96]. This phenomenon continued in the Ur III period.

Eridu was deserted when the Akkadians rose to power in the 24th century BCE, and it continued to be uninhabited when the Gutians finally brought about the collapse of the Akkadian Empire in the mid-22nd century BCE. The broader region appears to have emerged from these turbulent periods relatively unscathed, likely due to it being geographically isolated from the Akkadian homelands further north.

The Third Dynasty of Ur period at Sumer came to an end in the 20th century BCE, when tribes from the east – those of Elam and Sua – overran the region and conquered the city of Ur and surrounding area. The cult of Enlil was gravely affected by the conflicts, as many cult-centers in Mesopotamia were destroyed.[97] Even though the city was abandoned and ruined, the temple platform and structures continued to be used up to the 2nd millennium BCE. During this time a settlement grew a little less than a mile north of the temple area, likely inhabited by the priests of the cult of Enki that continued to flourish.[98]

---

[92] Carter, R. (2006) "Boat remains and maritime trade in the Persian Gulf during the sixth and fifth millennia BC." *Antiquity, 80* (307), 52 - 63.
[93] Oates, 1960
[94] Crawford, 2004
[95] Crawford, 2004
[96] Crawford, 2004
[97] De Graef, K., and Tavernier, J. (2012) *Susa and Elam. Archaeological, Philological, Historical and Geographical Perspectives.: Proceedings of the International Congress held at Ghent University, December 14-17, 2009*. Brill.
[98] Safar, 'Ali Muṣṭafa, and Lloyd, 1981

Even after the temple at Eridu was abandoned, in the minds of the people and their rulers in the region it was still important. Even during the reign of the Babylonian king Nebuchadnezzar II in the 6th century BCE, parts of the original temple were restored.[99] Beyond its covering by the desert dunes, the numinous aspects of Eridu were replicated elsewhere, with shrines to Enki appearing in other cities and miniature versions of the Khor el Nejeif lagoons built elsewhere.[100] The priesthood of Enki was even exported by the 2nd millennium Babylonian king Hammurabi, and through their records and stories the myth of Eridu has survived to this day as a place where civilization emerged from chaos.[101]

Control of the region later split into a number of groups, including the Assyrians and Babylonians, who would go on to dominate the region in the centuries before the Achaemenid Persian Empire crashed down upon them and conquered Mesopotamia in 539 BCE. With the resulting ups and downs of any city-state, Eridu lasted through to about the 6th century BCE when it was finally abandoned. Agricultural activity had long ceased in the area as the major watercourses shifted further away, and over time, the sand dunes of the desert encroached upon the site, covering the smaller mounds and masking the presence of the ruined city.

Eridu in the Modern Age

Iraq is a young country that emerged in the mid-20th century from vassalage to Britain, and before that were centuries of Ottoman rule.[102] The history of Iraq is rich in both splendors and sorrows. Its history featured the most gifted of civilizations, yet their tale is one of the most tragic. Up to the eve of the Gulf War, it was still possible to enter this world and see a way of life that had been preserved for thousands of years, since long before civilization – that of the *Ma'dan*, the Marsh Arabs. The Marsh Arabs live in villages that are made completely of reeds. These villages look much like the first settlements must have done; manmade islands in freshwater lagoons, where they still live by fishing, raising water buffalo, cutting the reed beds, and cultivating the rich soil along the shores with levees.[103] Their reed houses – some nearly 100 feet long – are still built in the same fashion as was depicted 5,000 years ago in the art of Sumer.[104] In the 1990s, the sectarian religious persecutions waged by Saddam Hussein's government forced many of the Marsh Arabs to leave their homes and abandon their traditional way of life. The Iraqi government diverted the Tigris and Euphrates rivers in a way that caused the marshes inhabited by the Ma'dan people to dry up, in turn causing their food supply to vanish.[105] This

---

[99] Crawford, 2004
[100] Crawford, 2004
[101] Smith, G. V. (1982) "The Concept of God/the Gods as King in the Ancient Near East and the Bible." *Trinity Journal*, 3 (1), 18 - 38.
[102] Simons, 2016
[103] Young, G. (2011) *Return to the marshes: life with the marsh Arabs of Iraq*. Faber and Faber.
[104] Young, 2011
[105] Young, 2011

ultimately resulted in a large percentage of them becoming refugees.

Due to its place in the religion and culture of Mesopotamia Eridu was much more than an early settlement; it has become part of the region's national heritage. Saddam Hussein liked to cast himself in the role of the ancient kings of Mesopotamia, and he was not subtle in attempting to foster his own mythology and link his reign to that of his supposed forebears.[106] He named army units after ancient Mesopotamian kings, aped their monumental building style, and even rebuilt Babylon using bricks inscribed with his own name, reminiscent of the rebuilding of Eridu by the kings of Ur.[107]

Today, Eridu is a lonely, windswept, and utterly abandoned place, despite being one of the most famous places in the history of Mesopotamia. Not only did the Sumerians believe that this was the site of Creation, the first land which arose from the primeval sea at the beginning of time, they also thought that it was here that kingship and political society first came down to earth, and that it was here that the arts of civilization were initially developed. Despite its association with the antediluvian kings, the city never seemed to have a political role, remaining primarily a religious site. At its heart was a sacred shrine which preceded all other cities in the region.

A key quality of civilization is continuity and a sense of rootedness – a sense of "belonging" to a place, and the aspect of continuity seen at Eridu is truly remarkable. People managed to settle and thrive in an inhospitable environment far from any main resources other than mud and created a religious center that remained sacred for many thousands of years. Eridu is also the site for one of the first examples of national mythmaking, serving as a place where Babylonians, Assyrians, Sumerians, and others could all point to as their place of origin. To them, Eridu was a place to feel proud of, symbolizing all the gifts bestowed upon them by the gods. Picking over the debris of Paradise, many of the archaeologists found proof of the Bible's stories – that the very beginning of the ascent to civilization was juxtaposed with evidence of its eventual fall.

Online Resources

Other books about ancient history by Charles River Editors

Other books about Eridu on Amazon

---

[106] Mackey, S. (2003) *The reckoning: Iraq and the legacy of Saddam Hussein.* WW Norton and Company.
[107] Mackey, 2003

Bibliography

Algaze, Guillermo. 1989. "The Uruk Expansion: Cross-cultural Exchange in Early Mesopotamian Civilization." *Current Anthropology* 30: 571-608.

Anthony, David W. 2007. *The Horse, the Wheel, and Language: How Bronze-Age Riders from the Eurasian Steppes Shaped the Modern World*. Princeton, New Jersey: Princeton University Press.

Curtis, J.E. and J.E. Reade, eds. 1995. *Art and Empire: Treasures from Assyria in the British Museum*. London: British Museum Press.

Dalby, Andrew. 1986. "The Sumerian Catalogs." *Journal of Library History* 21: 475-487.

Driel, G. van. 1995. "Nippur and the Inanna Temple during the Ur III Period." *Journal of the Economic and Social History of the Orient* 38: 393-406.

Fornara, Charles William. 1988. *The Nature of History in Ancient Greece and Rome*. Los Angeles: University of California Press.

Frankfort, Henri. 1996. *The Art and Architecture of the Ancient Orient*. New Haven, Connecticut: Yale University Press.

Green, Margaret Whitney (1975). Eridu in Sumerian Literature. Chicago: University of Chicago.

Kuhrt, Amélie. 2010. *The Ancient Near East: c. 3000-330 BCE*. 2 vols. London: Routledge.

Leick, Gwendolyn (2001). Mesopotamia: The invention of the city. London: Allen Lane. ISBN 0-7139-9198-4.

Macqueen, J.G. 2003. *The Hittites and Their Contemporaries in Asia Minor*. London: Thames and Hudson.

Mieroop, Marc van de. 2007. *A History of the Ancient Near East: ca. 3000-323 BCE*. 2nd ed. London: Blackwell.

Oates, Joan, "Ur and Eridu: the Prehistory", Iraq, 22

Oates, Joan (1960), Ur in Retrospect: In Memory of Sir C. Leonard Woolley, pp 32–50Kitchen, Kenneth A. 2003. *On the Reliability of the Old Testament*. Grand Rapids, Michigan: William B. Eerdmans.

Oppenheim, A. Leo (1998). Ancient Mesopotamia: Portrait of a dead civilization (Rev., 11th impr. ed.). Chicago: University of Chicago Press. ISBN 0-226-63187-7.

Pollock, Susan. 1999. *Ancient Mesopotamia: The Eden that Never Was*. Cambridge: Cambridge University Press.

Pritchard, James B, ed. 1992. *Ancient Near Eastern Texts Relating to the Old Testament*. 3rd ed. Princeton, New Jersey: Princeton University Press.

Sharlach, Tonia. 2007. "Social Change and the Transition from the Third Dynasty of Ur to the Old Babylonian Kingdoms c. 2112-1595 BCE." In *Regime Change in the Ancient Near East and Egypt: From Sargon of Agade to Saddam Hussein*, ed. Harriet Crawford, 61-72. Oxford: Oxford University Press.

———. 2005. "Diplomacy and the Rituals of Politics at the Ur III Court." *Journal of Cuneiform Studies* 57: 17-29

Sandars, Nancy K., ed. 1972. *The Epic of Gilgamesh*. Revised ed. London: Penguin Books.

Snell, Daniel C. 2011. *Religions of the Ancient Near East*. Cambridge: Cambridge University Press.

Soden, Wolfram von. 1994. *The Ancient Orient: An Introduction to the Study of the Ancient Near East*. Translated by Donald G. Schley. Grand Rapids, Michigan: William B. Eerdmans.

Speiser, E.A. 1983. "Ancient Mesopotamia." In *The Idea of History in the Ancient Near East*, ed. Robert C. Denton, 35-76. New Haven, Connecticut: American Oriental Society.

Vansina, Jan. 1985. *Oral Tradition as History*. Madison, Wisconsin: University of Wisconsin Press.

Verbrugge, Gerald P, and John M. Wickersham, eds. 2001. *Berossos and Manetho, Introduced and Translated: Native Traditions in Ancient Mesopotamia and Egypt*. Ann Arbor, Michigan: University of Michigan Press.

Ziskind, Jonathan R. 1972. "The Sumerian Problem." *History Teacher* 5: 34-41.

Free Books by Charles River Editors

We have brand new titles available for free most days of the week. To see which of our titles are currently free, click on this link.

Discounted Books by Charles River Editors

We have titles at a discount price of just 99 cents everyday. To see which of our titles are currently 99 cents, click on this link.

Printed in Dunstable, United Kingdom